The Anacondas in Life

How to Defeat the Obstacles That Hold You Back From Your Dreams and Your Potential

JAMES R. BALL

with JENNIFER A. KUCHTA

KEEP IT SIMPLE FOR SUCCESS®

The Anacondas in Life
How to Defeat the Obstacles That Hold You
Back from Your Dreams and Your Potential
ISBN: 1-887570-12-8

Published by The Goals Institute
www.goalpower.com
www.kissbooks.com
Email: info@goalsinstitute.com
703-264-2000

Keep It Simple for Success® is a registered trademark of
The Goals Institute.

Please contact us about volume discounts and
information about our keynotes, seminars, and train-the-
trainer resources on the contents of this book.

Printed in the United States of America

10 9 8 7 6 5 4 3 2 1

Dedication

Jim:

To my grandsons Ryan James Zinck and Tyler James Zinck.

I hope your lives will be free of Anacondas, full of joy, and abundant in love.

If you are ever stuck, just ask your Mom about the $1,000,000 I told her about so many times. That elusive million dollars always pulled her through and it will pull you through, too.

Jennifer:

To all of the people just starting in their careers after high school or college and to those individuals looking for a change.

I hope you are as fortunate as I have been and find your way to a career opportunity where you can work with passion and joy doing what you love in an Anaconda-Free Zone.

Welcome

The Anacondas in Life contains a message for living a happier and more successful life. This book will:

- Help you appreciate your capacity for greatness.
- Inspire you to imagine and pursue big dreams.
- Explain the obstacles that are holding you back from pursuing your dreams and potential.
- Teach you how to overcome those obstacles.
- Motivate you to take charge of your life and become all you can become.

Jim identified *The Anacondas in Life* in his first book, *Soar . . . If You Dare*®. This book expands on Jim's ideas, with more examples and tips, and is written in Jim's voice.

We hope this book helps you attain the success and joy you desire and deserve.

For information about our keynotes, seminars, and books, please visit us at www.goalpower.com.

Best wishes for joy and success!

James R. Ball

Jennifer A. Kuchta

Contents

Thanks

Thanks to Craig Cartwright for your incredible drawing of our now famous striking Anaconda. (manifest-stations.com)

Thanks to Ann Hunter at AAH Graphics, Inc. for your editorial input and help in polishing our words and the messages they carry. (aahgraphics.com)

Thanks to Julie Young at Young Design, Inc. for your graphics support on the cover. (youngdesign.com)

Please Note

The stories and examples in this book are based on circumstances I have read about or observed. I created fictitious names and altered facts to provide anonymity. Any similarities between the examples in this book and individuals and situations in real life are purely coincidental.

My comments in this book are based upon my experiences as a father, author, speaker, businessman, and teacher. My intent is to offer the best ideas I know and believe to be correct.

Nothing written here should be construed as an attempt to offer the kind of advice a counselor, psychiatrist, psychologist, or other similarly trained professional might provide.

The Anacondas in Life

The greatest obstacles you face in life
are the unseen snakes waiting in the
road ready to strike. To achieve success
and happiness you must learn how to
avoid them or defeat them.

Snake!

IMAGINE YOU look across to the other side of the room. On the floor next to the wall you see a huge snake coiled up in a pile that would fill the trunk of a car.

The snake sees you. It eases its head to the floor and begins to uncoil, stretch out, and slither your way.

The killer on the floor is no ordinary snake. It is an Anaconda, the largest, most powerful snake in the world. At maturity, the Anaconda stretches 37 feet, is as big around as a man, and weighs 450 pounds.

The Anaconda is a South American water snake and member of the boa constrictor family. Anacondas are stealth killers that anger easily. They devour 40 pounds of prey each day. Anacondas kill by wrapping their bone-crushing coils around a victim and squeezing until the prey cannot breathe and suffocates or is crushed to death and dies from internal bleeding. The snake then unhinges its jaws and swallows its victim whole.

Anacondas take away the breath of life and crush life's breath-taking moments.

You might be wondering what the image of the Anaconda inching toward you right now or the horrific picture of an Anaconda killing its prey has to do with you. The answer is *more than you may think*.

Anacondas Hold Us Back from Greatness

Greatness is a possibility for everyone. We all can improve our circumstances and lives.

Most people do not realize they are underachieving their potential and passing up dreams they could attain. They have no idea that undetected obstacles are holding them back from what they could become.

I identified these invisible obstacles years ago and called them the *Anacondas in Life* (the *Anacondas*). You may never detect them, but they are attacking you and working against you every day.

Individuals who learn how to recognize and avoid or defeat these Anacondas are able to fulfill their potential and achieve the dreams, happiness, and success they desire. People who do not learn how to recognize and defeat them will not attain the dreams, happiness, and success they could have.

It is impossible to overcome these barriers unless you understand what they are and have some idea how to conquer them. You cannot defeat enemies unless you know you have them.

> *Anacondas are not just people who are intentionally and obviously negative and mean. We all have a little Anaconda blood in us that we need to control.*
>
> —Jennifer Kuchta

What People Say About Their Anacondas

Here are some insights from people who have recognized the Anacondas in their lives.

- "I have so many Anacondas in my life it's not funny. I feel like an Anaconda magnet. I went to a party and some dude starts telling me about all the bad (expletive) in his life. I had to leave to get away."

- "Everyone at work hates it there."

- "My boyfriend is my worst Anaconda. When he tells me how stupid I am he totally ruins my day."

- "The woman in the cubicle next to me is the biggest whiner and complainer I have ever met. I hate going to work knowing she'll be there."

- "Every time I try something I get dumped on. I started reading about being vegetarian. My father rolled his eyes and said I was asinine."

- "My Mom couldn't wait to tell everyone our neighbor was laid off. She is so spiteful."

- "I don't need friends who talk behind my back."

- "When I listed who calls me instead of just me calling them I realized I had very few friends."

- "My father is *so* condescending. He treats me like I can't figure anything out for myself."

- "The only way I could get rid of the Anacondas in my life was to move away from my parents."

Anacondas Are Everywhere

If you are thinking you are safe because you do not live in the jungles of South America, think again. The Anacondas in Life live where you live, work where you work, exercise where you exercise, and belong to the same organizations as you.

The deceptive part is Anacondas do not look like snakes. They look like some of the people you know. A special species of Anaconda even looks like you!

How Anacondas Destroy

Anacondas work by attacking your beliefs and your aspirations. They choke your drive, enthusiasm, willpower, confidence, and sense of self-worth.

Anacondas say and do things that create negative, limiting thoughts. If you hear or replay these thoughts often enough, you begin to accept them as true and hardwire them into your brain. They become your realities and frame the world you see.

Eventually, instead of pursuing your dreams, you become content and pursue only those goals you think you can achieve. You avoid goals you do not think you can attain. You rise to the levels of your own expectations and beliefs and no farther.

The devastating aspect of this is you will not realize what happened. You will not realize you have lowered your expectations and aspirations. You will not realize you are aiming lower and hitting lower targets.

The 6 Anacondas in Life

THERE ARE NUMEROUS Anacondas in Life. I have identified six species:

1. Dream Snatchers
2. Limitation Thinking
3. Doubt and Despair
4. Undeservedness
5. Demotivators
6. You and Your Negative Self-Talk

These six Anaconda types come in all shapes and sizes. They can be people, places, events, and objects. Keep reading for descriptions and examples of these six Anacondas.

Be on the lookout for all of these beasts. As each species has its own unique crushing coils, you need to recognize and understand its threat and what you can do to avoid or overcome the negative and limiting impact it can have on your beliefs.

> *What you do not know can hurt you.*
> *What you do not know cannot help you.*

If you succeed in life, you must do it in spite of the efforts of others to pull you down. There is nothing in the idea that people are willing to help those who help themselves. People are willing to help a man who can't help himself, but as soon as a man is able to help himself, they join in making his life as uncomfortable as possible.

—Edgar W. Howe

Dream Snatchers

DREAM SNATCHERS are dream killers. They are Anacondas that snatch away dreams and crush happiness and hope.

Your dreams are all your desires and aspirations. They include your big dreams and long-term goals, like graduating from college and buying a house, and the smaller goals and ideas you pursue in everyday life, like losing five pounds and learning to play the guitar.

Triple Threat

Dream Snatchers pose a triple threat.

First, they threaten your dreams themselves and the goals you would achieve by pursuing them. When a Dream Snatcher snatches a dream from you, you do not pursue it. As a result, you underachieve and do not attain or become what you could.

Second, by snatching your dreams, Dream Snatchers rob you of happiness and hope. Your degree of happiness is dependent upon your degree of hope. You are happy when you are hopeful and you are unhappy when you lose hope.

Third, if Dream Snatchers snatch your dreams away often enough, you quit being a dreamer. You lower your sights and aspirations and keep them low.

Marge and the Marathon

MARGE SAYS she is thinking about running the Boston Marathon. Greg says, "Are you crazy? You don't have enough time to get in shape." Marge now has second thoughts and takes a pass on the race.

Greg just killed Marge's dream.

By snatching Marge's dream, Greg cheats her out of the benefits of getting into shape and the *lifetime* satisfaction and pride she would have had from knowing she completed the race.

Greg also takes away the happiness Marge would have enjoyed from looking forward to the race and completing it.

If Marge gets into a pattern of thinking about dreams and then setting them aside, she will become a quitter instead of an achiever.

By snatching Marge's marathon dream away, Greg pushes Marge toward a habit of talking about dreams instead of acting on them.

Greg is a Dream Snatcher.

Dream Snatchers Cause Complacency

Once you quit dreaming, you become apathetic, content, and complacent. You settle for less than you could have. You play it safe and avoid taking risks. You lose the wonderment you had as a child. You never stretch for the stars and achieve your potential.

A friend looked back ten years after college and remarked, "I am disappointed in myself. When I graduated, I was full of fire ready to achieve great things. I have settled for much less than my dreams. I'm complacent." This is the work of Dream Snatchers.

Dream Snatcher Evidence and Warning Signs

You know a Dream Snatcher has attacked you when someone says or does something that:

- Lets the air out of your balloon, bursts your bubble, or rains on your parade.
- Stomps on your idea or steals your thunder.
- Wipes the smile off your face.
- Kills your joy.
- Tramples your enthusiasm.
- Knocks the wind out of your sails.
- Shakes your confidence.
- Shatters your hopes.

Lucinda and Her Idea

LUCINDA, A NEW HIRE, surprised everyone at the weekly staff meeting by announcing a process she created for updating web pages. She passed out a summary and said, "I hope you like it."

Bob, a senior analyst, scowled and looked over his glasses. "Oh, *really*?" he said. He glanced at the sheet and shook his head.

Marcia, a manager, forced a smile and said, "You can't be serious. Do we really need a new process for updating web pages? And why would you be the one to design it if we did?"

No one said a word.

Lucinda had two Anacondas attacking her. Their weight and constricting coils were too much to bear. Tears welled up in her eyes.

Fortunately, Max, the department head, saved Lucinda. While looking down at Lucinda's sheet he said, "I don't know what you mean, Marcia. Creativity is not restricted to us old timers. Have any of you looked at this? It's pretty neat."

Lucinda's spirit soared. In that instant, her commitment to and trust in Max went from whatever it had been to way over 100%.

Can you recall a situation like the one in the *Lucinda and Her Idea* box, where you were a victim of Dream Snatchers? The problem is that there is not always someone like Max around who believes in dreams and dreamers and saves the day.

People Are Not Always Aware They Are Dream Snatchers

People often do not realize they are Dream Snatchers. They do not understand the damage they inflict on people they love. Here are some examples:

A little girl told her loving mother she wanted to become a ballerina only to have her mother become a Dream Snatcher with, "Honey that takes too much practice and lots of money we don't have."

I provided a keynote and a woman came up to me afterwards, crying. She said, "I realized after hearing you speak that I have been an Anaconda to my children all their lives. I am going to change, starting now."

A bright new salesman said he intended to exceed his sales quota by 20%. Then he looked across the room to see his Dream Snatching sales manager roll his eyes to the person next to him.

An executive told me after a seminar, "I never realized how much of an Anaconda I am to my husband. I am always making fun of his business ideas and attempts. It never occurred to me that I could be hurting him or killing his dreams. How awful I have been."

Techniques of Dream Snatchers

Dream Snatchers use a variety of techniques to crush ideas, hopes, and dreams. They roll their eyes, laugh or smile in a condescending manner, smirk, and scowl. Dream Snatchers *say* things like:

- "You can't be serious."
- "That's ridiculous."
- "You're wearing rose-colored glasses."
- "Who are you kidding?"
- "Don't count your chickens."
- "Why would you want to do that?"
- "Maybe some day." (But not now.)
- "Who's filling your head with that silliness?"
- "Quit chasing windmills."
- "Get your feet on the ground."
- "Don't get your hopes up."
- "Right." (Sarcastically.)

Dream Snatching by Indifference

A person does not have to be cynical and negative to be a Dream Snatcher. Dream Snatchers also kill dreams by being withdrawn, unmoved, cold-hearted, inattentive, disinterested, and emotionless. Individuals who act bored and apathetic kill ideas and sap joy quickly.

An example is when a little boy runs in to show his father a picture he has drawn only to have his father say, "Not now Timmy, Daddy's watching the game."

A famous entertainer told how his father never listened to his music or attended a concert until late in the singer's career. He choked up when he said he waited nearly 40 years to hear his father's approval and praise. Sadly, his father passed away a few months later.

The teacher who never calls on Jolina, or the coach who never gives Raul the chance to play shows another form of indifference. When parents, teachers, and coaches do not give individuals a chance to demonstrate their abilities and worth, they are Dream Snatchers.

In business, Dream Snatchers sometimes kill dreams by putting up roadblocks. A manager who never finds time to approve new ideas is a Dream Snatcher. A co-worker who says, "Shouldn't we check with Ed?" could be a Dream Snatcher, too.

Ridicule Is a Dream Snatcher's Specialty

One of the techniques Dream Snatchers like is ridicule. Ridicule is the malicious and bitter belittling, mocking, or scorning of someone's dreams or ideas. Ridicule often is in the form of a patronizing remark.

> *Ridicule is the weapon most feared by enthusiasts of every description.*
>
> —Sir Walter Scott

Who Is Smiling Now?

HERE IS the story a young entrepreneur relates:

"When I was just starting my home-based business everyone in my family joked about it constantly. At Thanksgiving dinner, my older brother laughed and laughed. He said I had to start a business because I was the only person who would hire me.

"I went home that night even more intent on being successful. And I was.

"Now I am the one who is laughing. Only I'm not laughing, really. I'm just glad I stuck with it. In hindsight, my brother's joking about my business actually spurred me onward. It was a good thing in a strange way. I love my brother, but he sure was mean. I don't know why. Maybe he was jealous."

The Fragility of Dreams and Ideas

Dreams are fragile and delicate. They are easily shattered and destroyed, particularly in their early stages when you are just forming them in your mind.

When you are developing your dreams, you are energized and excited; however, you must build momentum and bolster your confidence to keep going.

Anacondas do not always attack dreams with full force. Sometimes they start coiling around your dreams with one small negative remark and then increase the intensity of their attack a little at a time until they eventually weigh you down and bring you to a stop.

Anacondas are extremely persistent in waiting you out. They can be like barnacles that attach to the hull of a ship. Over time they multiply, and it takes more energy and effort to pull them along. If they simply do nothing to help you, encourage you, or acknowledge your ideas, Dream Snatchers will use their indifference to drag you and your dreams to the bottom of the sea.

> *You see children know such a lot now,*
> *they soon don't believe in fairies, and*
> *every time a child says, 'I don't believe*
> *in fairies,' there is a fairy somewhere*
> *that falls down dead.*
>
> —from *Peter Pan*
> by James Matthew Barrie

Key Strategy for Overcoming Dream Snatchers

There is one overriding strategy to use when it comes to Dream Snatchers: **Ignore them and press on to pursue your dreams**.

One of my favorite examples of someone ignoring Dream Snatchers is Michael Flatley, the dancer.

When interviewed, Flatley said, "I can go back to when I was six years old. I was always getting in trouble for dreaming, and the things I got in trouble for dreaming are the things I am doing today."

Flatley kept visualizing his dreams, "in full living color" as he put it. Now, his dreams are his reality.

Michael Flatley refused to allow Dream Snatchers to dampen his spirits or crush his dreams. Thank goodness he did or none of us would ever have seen *Riverdance* or his fabulous follow-on productions, *Lord of the Dance* and *Celtic Tiger*.

> *Hold fast to dreams*
> *For if dreams die*
> *Life is a broken-winged bird*
> *That cannot fly*
> *Hold fast to your dreams*
> *For when dreams go*
> *Life is a barren field*
> *Frozen with snow.*

> —Langston Hughes

Dream Snatchers
Dos and Don'ts

Do:

- Be prepared for Dream Snatchers.
- Ignore Dream Snatchers.
- Hold on to your dreams and pursue them.
- Follow your bliss.
- Dare to dream.
- Dream big.
- Transform your dreams into goals and plans.
- Take action to move your dreams forward.
- Visualize attaining your dreams.
- Go all out for your dreams.
- Seek support from those who believe in you.

Don't:

- Be a Dream Snatcher.
- Let a Dream Snatcher get to you.
- Give up on your dreams.
- Listen to Dream Snatchers.

Every time you state what you want or believe, you're the first to hear it. It's a message to both you and others about what you think is possible. Don't put a ceiling on yourself.

—Oprah Winfrey

Limitation Thinking

LIMITATION THINKING exists when you let anything restrict your beliefs about who you are and lower your aspirations about what you can become.

Your beliefs create an immovable mental barrier that limits your potential by defining what is possible and what is not. To achieve your dreams and pursue your greatness you must leap from impossibility thinking into the world of possibility thinking.

The Invisible Fence

Have you ever watched a dog encounter one of those invisible radio-controlled fences?

When the unsuspecting dog strays near the concealed fence, it gets an electric jolt from the metal tag on its neck. Instantly, the dog yelps and jerks back.

Once shocked, the dog never tries to cross that spot again. In a short time, the dog mentally marks the perimeter of the yard where the concealed fence lies buried. Eventually, the fence does not have to be on to work. The dog never forgets; it has hardwired in memory each painful jolt around the yard.

People are the same and apply the adage, "once burned, twice shy." Once we encounter limitations, especially painful or embarrassing jolts that knock us back, we mentally record them and remember them unwaveringly. It is almost impossible for us to go beyond limitations we have hardwired into our long-term memories. The most damaging aspect is that we do not realize we have allowed our own thoughts to build invisible walls around our outlook. You can become a Limitation Thinker without knowing it!

Going back to the invisible fence, the yard is that dog's world. It is the extent of its existence. It will not venture beyond to explore what else is out there.

When humans encounter obstacles and setbacks they too, establish mental boundaries. After striking out a few times, instead of following the adage, *try and try again,* many people hit the bench and never come back to bat.

Once we get comfortable existing within our self-defined boundaries, we tend to stay there. We forget there is a bigger world we could pursue and attain. Like the dog in its yard, we do not venture down the street to see what is there. Yet, there is much to see and enjoy.

Distorted Realities

In addition to creating barriers from setbacks and disappointments, people erect mental barriers around distorted facts or untruths they have accepted as truths.

An example is the common comment, "Girls aren't good at math." This statement is not true, yet many women have mental barriers about math because they encoded these limiting thoughts in childhood.

My friend took her daughter, Susan, in for a physical. The doctor asked Susan what new subjects she would be taking. "Geometry," Susan said.

The doctor scrunched up her nose. "Geometry. Ugh! I had trouble with geometry. I think all girls do."

As predicted, Susan did poorly in geometry. Was it because girls aren't good at math? Or, was it because the doctor did not realize the damage her words could do? The chances of a fifteen-year-old *not* believing what her doctor says are remote.

Techniques of Limitation Thinkers

Limitation Thinkers use many techniques to put boundaries around your dreams. They say things like:

- "Be realistic," or "Let's get real here."
- "Don't rock the boat."
- "Fat chance."
- "That's out of my league."
- "Be practical."
- "We'll make do with what we have."
- "There is no money in the budget for this."
- "We're content with what we have."
- "That's pie in the sky."

In business the two most common expressions Limitation Thinkers use are "Be realistic" and "We've always done it that way."

I can tell you from experience that the word *realistic* when used to establish goals is a clever and disguised substitute for the words "easy" and "low."

The new manager of an organization jokingly said he got stomach cramps from hearing "We've always done it that way," when he kept asking why things were being done the way they were being done.

Limitation Thinkers like to be the first ones to point out why something will not work. The faster they can shoot down an idea, the better they feel.

Unfortunately, Limitation Thinkers who revel in shooting down ideas quickly are a big obstacle to improving performance, profits, and creativity. It is easy to shoot down an idea; anyone can. The people who make the real contribution are those who try to find out what is right about an idea and put it to use.

Limitation Thinkers Are Change Resisters

The big problem with change management initiatives is that the people in management responsible for making changes often are the very people who resist change the most.

People who resist change are Anaconda Limitation Thinkers and often do not realize it.

That's Funny. Real Funny.

WHEN BEGINNING a goal-setting retreat, board members of an association said they wanted to think outside the box and make changes.

During the discussion, I suggested a dues increase to pay for new programs they wanted. Here are the comments I heard *immediately*:

- "No way."
- "Members will drop like crazy."
- "That's funny, Jim. Real funny. Have you seen our member retention rates?"
- "We tried that two years ago. I thought we would never hear the end of it."
- "I'm not signing that letter."

Guess what happened? The organization increased membership dues 20%. The resistance of members to a dues increase was not from the size of the dues, it was from the lack of services and value provided. Members were willing to pay more for better services they valued.

The key point from the above goal-setting retreat story is this: Even though each person said he or she was for change, not a single board member was in favor of the dues increase when I first suggested it. *Initially, every person vigorously resisted a dues increase.*

If you encounter Limitation Thinkers and want to overcome them, you have to be prepared to persist with conviction. If I had backed down, even a little, the board members would have voted down a dues increase.

Change Resistance by Inertia

If you want change, a force you are going to have to overcome is *inertia*. Inertia is the tendency of people to want to continue what they have been doing the way they have been doing it.

Many people say, "If you keep on doing what you have been doing, you are going to keep on getting the results you have been getting." This is not true. If you keep on doing what you have been doing, you are going to fall behind because others will improve and pass you.

A key principle for change management is this: *Coasting is always a downhill proposition.* This principle applies to both organizations and individuals. If you ever find yourself coasting, just be aware that someone else is not.

> *An American figure skater had trouble getting up every morning at 5:00 to train . . . until she placed a photo of the Russian champion on her alarm. Under the picture were the words: "Comrade, while you were sleeping, I was training."*

—Ron Gilbert

Limitation Thinking Stranglehold

Most people trapped within walls of Limitation Thinking do not know they are trapped there, and many adamantly deny they are being close-minded.

Rigid Thinking

A YOUNG MAN said there was "zero chance" he would ever be able to change the ineffective and bureaucratic way his organization operated.

"You can't really believe that," I said. "If you and others want to make changes, you can. You could be the catalyst to changing your entire organization."

"Let me put it the way I tell everyone else," he said with a tone. "If I had a straw I would have a better chance of sucking the Potomac River dry than I would of changing the way management does things in my organization."

This young man had told this same victim story so many times there was no way I was going to change what he thought. He had programmed himself with an immovable wall of limiting thoughts. He was suffocating in his own Anaconda stranglehold. There was nothing I could say or do to help him. Some people do not want to be helped and he was one of them. I moved the conversation to another topic.

Your Thoughts Are Your Instructions

The words you think and say are not just words; they are instructions.

When you repeat words and thoughts, you are encoding them into memory. If you say a limiting phrase often enough, your brain treats that thought as a set of instructions that you use to create your realities.

The managing partner of an accounting firm told me, "There is no way I will ever be able to convince my partners they should provide monthly performance assessments and feedback for associates."

I told her that as long as she felt that way, she was correct. Her thoughts set her own limit. Her words were precise predictors of her future.

The concept that we are what we think has been around and accepted as a fundamental truth for many, many years.

> *All that we are is the result of what we have thought. The mind is everything. What we think, we become.*
>
> —Prince Gutama Siddhartha

Breaking Free of What You Know

Sometimes you know too much and need to break free of your own intellect. What you know, or think you know, creates an invisible barrier that keeps you from seeing or considering something new. The adage, "You can't see the forest for the trees," is true.

Several types of Limitation Thinkers are specialists at being closed-minded.

Know-it-alls think they know everything there is to know. You cannot tell them anything.

Not invented here is a *groupthink* weakness that forms in many organizations.

I can do it by myself is a weakness some individuals have. By refusing to accept ideas or assistance from anyone, they limit their knowledge and results.

What if I Gave You $1,000,000?

A technique I use to help individuals get beyond their own intellect is to ask them to pretend so that they can reframe their minds and see things differently. An easy way to accomplish this is to pretend you have a million dollars to solve the problem. This always stirs innovative thinking. *See* the example with my daughter described in the box on the next page.

What if I Gave You $1,000,000?

MY DAUGHTER Jennifer opened her package for graduate school and realized her application was late. Near tears, she said, "Dad, the letter says it was due February 10th—No exceptions!"

The rules were Jennifer's limiting thoughts.

I pondered and said, "Jennifer, what if I gave you a million . . ."

Jennifer said, "Dad, please don't do this."

What does a father do when the world crashes down on his daughter? I said, "Jennifer, what would you do if I gave you a million dollars to get into the university this fall?"

Jennifer fought tears. "Dad, I hate this."

"I know you hate it. But what if I gave you a million dollars to get in school? Humor me."

Jennifer sat in silence. I could see her mind shifting gears. Then it happened. The tension in her face vanished. She began, "I guess the first thing I would do is call the Registrar's office."

"Good idea. Then what?" I said.

Jennifer was on a roll. Instead of replaying her limiting thoughts, she was thinking outside the box to develop a workable plan. Jennifer entered the doctoral program at Virginia Tech that fall. The university made an exception.

Limitation Thinking
Dos and Don'ts

Do:

- Think, "What's possible?" "What could I do?"
- Recognize that your thoughts create invisible barriers that restrict and limit your goals and dreams.
- Focus on the future, and focus onward and upward.
- Use the technique *What if I gave you $1,000,000?*
- Recognize that the first reaction of almost everyone is to resist change and new ideas.
- Focus on the facts, not your feelings about the facts.
- Take some risks and have new experiences.
- Listen to and be receptive to the ideas of others.

Don't:

- Be an impossibility thinker.
- Dwell on the present and the past.
- Try to change someone who vehemently resists change, innovation, and new ideas.
- Coast or become content.
- Resist help if it is offered.
- Try to find reasons it won't or can't work; instead find reasons it might or will work.

If you lose hope, somehow you lose the vitality that keeps life moving, you lose that courage to be, that quality that helps you go on in spite of it all. And so today I still have a dream.

—Martin Luther King, Jr.

Doubt and Despair

DOUBT AND DESPAIR are twin Anacondas that attack confidence and the will to act. Doubt attacks belief and despair attacks hope. Together they crush your faith in the future of what you may achieve and become.

Doubt and Despair are specialists at pointing out obstacles and what can go wrong. They place monkeys of misgiving on your back. They wring their hands chanting how bad it is or how bad it is going to become.

The venomous words of Doubt and Despair make you lose confidence and hold back. You second guess yourself, become overly cautious, procrastinate, keep rethinking things, and avoid taking action.

The Fear of Failure and a "No" Answer

The fear of failure is an obstacle you create in your mind by imagining the rejection and disappointment you may feel if the event you fear actually happens.

A common example is the fear of hearing a *no*. A woman allowed her fear of a no to keep her from applying for a new position. She said, "I kept thinking, what will happen if I do not get it?"

The fear of a no routinely keeps sales professionals and individuals seeking jobs or promotions from taking action. When they hear a no in their minds, they get disappointed, afraid, and stop their pursuit.

People rationalize to avoid getting a no. I asked a sales associate who his ten best prospects were, and he told me. He had not called on them, and I asked why. He said he was saving his best prospects because if he called on them and they said no, then he would no longer have ten good prospects.

Techniques of Doubt and Despair

The Anacondas of Doubt and Despair erect barriers of concern by saying things like:

- "Never take a risk you can avoid."
- "Don't hold your breath."
- "Better safe than sorry."
- "Nothing ventured, nothing lost."
- "What can go wrong will go wrong."
- "There is uncertainty around every corner."
- "Play it safe."

For the Anacondas of Doubt and Despair, the time is never right. There is never enough information. There is always some excuse for waiting, abandoning the goal, or postponing action to another day.

When we think of failure, failure will be ours. Never think of failure for what we think will come about.

—Maharishi Mahesh Yogi

The Lingering Doubt

When someone or something plants doubt in your mind, you will focus on the doubt.

This is a huge problem since people tend to act out their dominant thoughts.

Doubt causes athletes and others to choke. A young man said he was so concerned with being rejected during an interview that he said and did things to self-destruct.

Many people who say they want to pursue bigger goals talk themselves out of those big goals before they ever get started because of the Anaconda of Doubt.

Self-Destruction at the Piano Recital

Once the thought of failure enters the brain, the tendency to self-destruct has fertile ground to grow and become a dominate instruction.

When my daughters were kids, their piano instructor talked me into participating in their piano recital to show my support for them. As I watched the children play their selections all I could think about was how stupid I was going to look as the only adult playing in the recital—a child's piece at that.

When it was my turn to play, my fingers turned to wood. Words cannot describe it. My doubt and fear took control. I played as poorly as I imagined I would.

Doubt Can Destroy You

An overpowering and all encompassing sense of doubt can be destructive.

One smart young man could never pass the CPA exam because he was always afraid he would fail.

The fear of failure itself can kill. A business owner committed suicide because he was afraid of impending financial disaster. I had a friend who killed himself when he was having trouble with his career.

> *I have never known a man who died
> from overwork, but many who died
> from doubt.*
>
> —Charles W. Mayo

Despair

Some people are not happy unless they are talking about how miserable they are. I met a man once whose response to everything was, "life sucks."

Anacondas of Despair are doomsayers, naysayers, and worrywarts. They kill dreams and derail ideas with comments of distress and concern.

If you try to imagine solving all of the problems before you start, you will never begin.

In life, there are only so many days. People who put off pursuing their dreams until tomorrow often end up putting them off forever.

Strategies for Overcoming Doubt and Despair

When it comes to overcoming Doubt and Despair, the goal is to alter your "inner voice" by replacing doubt and despair with thoughts of belief and hope.

When in Doubt, Cast It Out

A must-do step for dealing with Doubt and Despair is to remove the negative thoughts from your mind and replace them with positive thoughts. See the chapter, *You and Your Own Negative Self-Talk*, for ideas and suggestions on how to do this.

Avoid Anacondas of Doubt and Despair

One of the best techniques for overcoming Doubt and Despair is to avoid or remove the source. If an individual is causing you to be overly concerned about your goals, quit spending time with that person. If you have an Anaconda of Doubt on your team, sometimes you need to get that snake off the team.

Keep Hope Alive

The most important strategy for overcoming Doubt and Despair is to do whatever it takes to keep hope alive.

Everyone has a little doubt or despair occasionally. That is not a bad thing. What is bad is allowing yourself to focus on the downside so intently that you erase all traces of belief and hope. Things are never so bad that it is hopeless. There is always tomorrow. It is only hopeless if we think it is hopeless. Nothing is over until we call it quits.

"Separated from Payroll"

ON A BIG project, Cory was our resident Anaconda of Doubt and Despair. He brought us down at each progress meeting.

Cory always focused on the things that had not gone right. He loved to point out upcoming obstacles that could set us back.

Despite the project manager's efforts to encourage Cory to be optimistic instead of pessimistic, Cory went out of his way to emphasize the negative. Cory's favorite omen was that we would not finish the project on time "without an amazing miracle of some kind." This went on for weeks.

Then one week I went to the progress meeting and Cory was missing. I asked where he was. The project manager said, "It was 'an amazing miracle of some kind'. Cory has been separated from payroll."

Doubt and Despair
Dos and Don'ts

Do:

- Cast out doubt—imagine reaching inside your brain, grabbing the doubt and throwing it out.
- Focus your attention on the results you want.
- Eliminate *I can't* from your vocabulary.
- Repeat to yourself, *I can . . . I can do this.*
- Quit thinking about what could go wrong.
- Take action to accomplish what you desire.
- Change subjects away from doom and gloom.
- Remember there is always tomorrow.

Don't:

- Listen to Anacondas of Doubt and Despair.
- Hang around people who are constantly raising concerns and reminding you of the risks.
- Allow anyone to put a monkey of doubt, concern, or misgiving on your back.
- Quit or think about quitting.
- Allow yourself to focus on what you do not want to happen; focus instead on what you want to happen.
- Lose hope or take away someone else's hope.

If we treat people as they are, we make them worse. If we treat people as they ought to be, we help them become what they are capable of becoming.

—Johann Wolfgang von Goethe

Undeservedness

UNDESERVEDNESS is an Anaconda that attacks self-esteem and the sense of self-worth and value. It erodes your confidence in your ability to achieve your goals and cope with the challenges of everyday life.

Undeservedness is a debilitating snake because you only pursue and achieve what you believe you deserve to attain based upon your own self-assessment.

You Get What You *Think* You Deserve

The adage, "you get what you deserve" does not make sense. No one sat in judgment when you were born and said, "This is what you deserve."

Unfortunately, this principle is the way life works:

You get what you *think* you deserve.

Individuals rarely achieve or become more than what they think they deserve.

Childhood Sets the Stage

Your childhood experiences established the foundation for your self-beliefs and what you think you deserve.

When children are hugged, praised, applauded, read to, and cared for properly they develop a strong sense of self and a high sense of self-worth.

When children are criticized, beaten, bullied, teased, ignored, and yelled at they develop negative images of themselves and a low sense of self-worth.

Nurturing of Adults

Your adult experiences and environment also affect your self-esteem and what you think you deserve.

If Bruce praises Rene for doing good work, thanks her for her suggestions, pays attention when she talks, listens to her opinions, and gives her big assignments, Rene is going to feel good about herself.

If Stella criticizes Darryl for making mistakes, nags at him to pick up the pace, yells at him because he does not do it her way, and ignores him during meetings, Darryl is going to feel down and bad about himself.

You Are Worthy!

It sometimes is hard to believe we are worthy.

In a *20/20* special on *Winning*, Drew Carey, the comedian and new host of *The Price Is Right*, described how he suffered from the "I am not worthy" trap when growing up. At age eighteen, he tried to kill himself. He rationalized that he was not worthy of having the fun and success his friends were having.

My entire first year in public accounting I thought I was not worthy of my job. My secret was that I feared I would be fired once the firm figured out it had made a mistake hiring me. Fortunately, over time I built up my self-confidence and sense of worth.

I recommend you quit thinking you are not worthy. Get going to make things happen. Start achieving results that will build your confidence.

Effort Is Required

A misconception is thinking that people are lucky or predestined for happiness and wealth. Although some people like Prince William and Lisa Presley were born into families of wealth and fame, most of us were not.

The good news is that most famous and successful people worked to get what they have.

Tiger Woods was not born famous and wealthy. He became famous and wealthy because he has been golfing and improving his game since he was six.

Effort is required. As the principal of an inner city high school put it, "Everyone wants a diploma, but not everyone wants to do the work."

Don't Let Yourself Go

Self-image and pride are linked together. When you feel good about how you look, you feel good about yourself and what you deserve. A good set of clothes and a neat haircut can do wonders for self-esteem.

It is hard for you to believe you deserve success if the reflection in the mirror shows that you have let yourself go.

If you want to boost your feelings about what you deserve, start by taking better care of yourself and treating yourself better.

Press for excellence, too. People who take pride in their work reason that they deserve the best because they did their best.

Overcoming Feelings of Undeservedness

How can you change what you think you deserve? The answer is simple. Do not sit in self-judgment.

None of us has any idea what we can achieve and become until we try. Whatever we have done, achieved, or experienced has no bearing on what we can achieve and become. We cannot change the past, but we get to create the future.

Somewhere in everyone is the spirit for greatness. Your job is to find that spirit and bring it forth. Life is not about determining what you deserve. Life is about going on a quest for the truth of what you can become.

You Deserve the Best

Whatever you *think* you deserve right this moment, you deserve even more.

No one sits in judgment of you and determines what you do and do not deserve to get out of life.

You deserve the very best in life, and you can choose what that is, and get it!

Undeservedness
Dos and Don'ts

Do:

- Remember you deserve whatever you are willing to work to get.
- Recognize that you have greatness within yourself, and your job is to find it and bring it forth.
- Take pride in your work and yourself.
- Put in the effort required to get what you want.
- Avoid Anacondas of Undeservedness that make you question what you deserve in life.

Don't:

- Think you do not deserve what you want. You do deserve what you want.
- Judge yourself.
- Judge others.
- Let others judge you.
- Let yourself go.

When you feel dog tired at night, it may
be because you growled all day.

—Author unknown

Demotivators

DEMOTIVATORS are Anacondas that bring us down.

To illustrate their diversity, six groups of Demotivators are listed below and described on the pages that follow.

Whiners include crabbers, complainers, faultfinders, grumblers, naggers, spoilsports, nitpickers, bellyachers, and killjoys.

Slackers include goof-offs, loafers, parasites, leeches, and freeloaders.

Victims include poor losers, bad sports, blamers, soreheads, and "woe-is-me" experts.

Bullies include intimidators, troublemakers, cynics, misanthropes, meanies, and unkind, spiteful, and hateful people.

Gossipers include back-stabbers, rumormongers, tattletales, and told-you-sos.

Agitators are people who are rude, impolite, and ill-mannered, and who do not follow the rules.

Dead Battery!

Have you ever gone to work with a fully charged battery of positive energy? Then someone starts whining, griping, and complaining. In no time, you feel drained, sapped, and stressed. A Demotivator has drained your battery!

Whiners

Whiners are always griping, complaining, and nagging about something. "Isn't this weather terrible?" "I have too much to do." "The service here is so bad." "Look at the price of that gas!" "My computer is so slow." "I hate cleaning." Whiners grumble about their problems, how difficult things are, how life is hard, and how bad things are, *for them*.

These Demotivators are active and vocal. They suck the energy and zap the enthusiasm out of everyone they encounter. Just one active Anaconda like this in an office can bring everyone down.

Oh That Traffic!

A WOMAN complained about the terrible traffic she had to endure. With fanfare, she began complaining as soon as she arrived every day.

She was having such a negative affect on co-workers, the president of the company asked her on several occasions to quit complaining. The woman continued grumbling, so the president asked her to leave. "She was just getting on everyone's nerves and was so disruptive. Everyone has the same traffic problems and she just made them seem worse. I had to do something," the president said.

Slackers

Slackers avoid work or do as little as possible. One slacker smiled and said, "I do just enough to get by. I'm going to put in my 25 years and then I am out of here."

Slackers often are so obvious at shirking work that the people near them start to wonder why they should put in a full day's effort and try so hard.

Victims

Victims dramatize their challenges and create an aura that they are sufferers to be pitied. Victims:

- See their glass as half empty or empty.
- Moan that they have been mistreated and are misunderstood.
- Blame others for their problems or shortcomings.
- Make excuses for not doing what they could be doing to change their lives.
- Feel no one is paying attention to them or appreciates them.

While some Victims need professional help, others are merely dramatizing their Victim role to get attention.

I know a woman who spends much of her time telling people about her troubles just so everyone will pay attention to her and feel sorry for her. Sadly, everyone close to her knows her game. They call her "Chicken Little" and make fun of her behind her back.

Sometimes we can turn ourselves around quickly when we realize we have become Victims.

Supernatural Turnaround

A WONDERFUL example of someone who was a Victim for a short period and then turned himself and his life around is Carlos Santana.

In the 1990s when his record sales were in a slump and he was without a contract, Carlos Santana was feeling sorry for himself. He remarked something to the effect that the world was against him.

The person Santana was with told him he was mistaken if he thought everyone was against him or out to get him. He explained that people were too busy with their own problems and lives to be worrying about what Carlos Santana was or was not doing.

This remark made Santana stop and think. He realized how absurd it was to think that the whole world was against him. Santana said that his reward for listening and changing his outlook was his album, *Supernatural*.

Supernatural was a phenomenal best seller. It marked the turning point and beginning of a steep upward trajectory in Santana's career. His success and music are legendary.

Bullies

Bullies are individuals who go out of their way to be mean and intimidate others. They build themselves up by tearing others down.

Technology has provided bullies with new tools and has stimulated some people who were not bullies before to become unseen Anacondas that strike from a distance.

Email and blogs are favorite tools of bullies. Some individuals create web pages to hurt others. Secretly capturing pictures and videos with cell phones and posting them on the Internet is a popular way to bully.

High school bullies now supplement in-person teasing and taunting with hate email campaigns and hate websites complete with pictures and videos. In one reported case the bullying got so bad, the victim committed suicide. Some cities have passed laws against bullying on the Internet.

In office settings, some individuals send poison email notes to people. Anacondas say hurtful things in digital format they would never dare to say in person.

Gossipers

Gossipers attack the reputation, pride, and self-esteem of individuals. They waste resources because their gossiping drains energy, reduces teamwork and cooperation, and directs effort away from results.

A gossiper is a person who enjoys broadcasting news about someone's personal affairs and problems.

Gossipers deal in negative and sensitive information. They constantly are on the prowl for intimate details they can peddle to others. "Did you hear Mona and her husband are having a tiff?" "Someone said Rick got in over his head financially with that big new house. Did you hear anything?" "Is Sonia off her diet? She looks like maybe she put on a few pounds."

Agitators

Agitators create annoyance by what they say and do and the way they say and do it. They are Demotivators because they sap our energy and enthusiasm.

Some agitators know they are irritating; others do not. Oftentimes it is not that agitators do any one big thing that is upsetting; rather, it is that they are constantly doing many little annoying things.

A woman said that some days she goes home feeling like she has been "picked to death by sparrows." Little things all day long can accumulate into a very stressful and exhausting day.

> *There is no excuse for being rude, disrespectful, arrogant, impolite, vulgar, selfish, or unkind.*
>
> —Jim Ball

Dealing with Demotivators

The three main strategies I use for dealing with Demotivators are to confront them, learn to ignore or avoid them, or dump them.

Confront Them

I am not a confrontational person; however, there are some cases where confrontation is my first choice for dealing with a Demotivator.

For example, if Brock drinks more than his share of the coffee, but never makes fresh coffee for others, I would ask him to either start taking turns making coffee or quit drinking it. This assumes that the approach in the office is for everyone to take a fair turn.

Learn to Ignore or Avoid Them

Since so many people have become rude and impolite, I now put up with and ignore many Demotivator-type annoyances that formerly would have gotten to me.

For example, if a woman on the treadmill next to me at the health club is using her cell phone even though cell phones are not permitted on the exercise floor, I would move to another machine rather than confront her. Policing the club's rules is not my job. After all, I am only going to be there an hour and I am not going to let her bother me.

Dump Them

A key technique I use for dealing with Demotivators is to dump them. If people are intent on being negative, I do not try to change them. When I try to motivate negative persons, they may end up demotivating me instead of me motivating them. So, when I encounter negative situations I often just move on.

For example, I joined a group created for business owners to share ideas and help each other. Instead of offering encouragement and nurturing advice, members of the group attacked each other and pointed out deficiencies. I dropped out of the group the next day and never once regretted it.

Never Feel Sorry for Yourself

Here is an essential rule for defeating Demotivators and being positive: **Never feel sorry for yourself.**

I do not believe in feeling sorry for myself. That accomplishes nothing good and makes things worse. Sometimes, however, it is good to vent and let out anger and frustration. If you need to release your depression or sadness, I recommend a *Five-Minute Pity Party*.

Once I had a pity party at night after everyone had gone to bed. I stepped out to our backyard and looked up at the stars. Then I talked aloud about my troubles and how bad things seemed. After I rambled a few minutes I said, "Okay, you got that off your chest, now go to bed."

That may sound silly, but I felt better.

Demotivators
Dos and Don'ts

Do:

- Take action to avoid Demotivators.
- Allow yourself a Five-Minute Pity Party if you need it.
- Learn to ignore Demotivators.
- Dump or avoid Demotivators that get to you.
- Take control.

Don't:

- Feel sorry for yourself.
- Be a Whiner, Slacker, Victim, Bully, Gossiper, or Agitator.
- Use email, the Internet, or other technologies to say or do anything you would not say or do in person.
- Demotivate anyone for any reason.

If you realized how powerful your thoughts are, you would never think a negative thought.

—Peace Pilgrim

You and Your Negative Self-Talk

THE WORST Anaconda of them all, the most damaging, and the deadliest . . . can be you!

When you think, "I hate Mondays" or "what a lousy week it's going to be," you are getting ready to anticipate and produce a bad Monday and a lousy week. If you say these things aloud, share them with others, or think them repeatedly, they become stronger commands that take control of your behavior to ensure that your Monday and week are awful.

When you say, "I can't lose weight," "I'll never get ahead," "I can't get out of debt," "I'm not lucky," or "I'll never amount to anything," you are winding your own mental Anaconda coils around your positive can-do spirit and crushing it dead.

How Negative Self-Talk Programs Your Brain

When you say or think things like, "I'm not good with computers" or "I'm overwhelmed," you are committing yourself to act out the images that those thoughts produce.

Author Marilyn Grey puts it this way: "Your brain doesn't know you're kidding. Random thoughts such as 'This job makes me sick' are viewed by the brain as instructions and you will implement those instructions."

Examples of Negative Self-Talk

Sometimes people say or think things they do not realize are negative or limiting thoughts. Below are examples of negative self-talk phrases I recommend you eliminate from your mind and self-talk.

- I can't.
- I don't have time.
- I might as well give up.
- I'm uncoordinated.
- I'm too old.
- I've got too much to do.
- I'm in a rut.
- I hate my life.
- I should just quit.
- Nothing goes right.
- She doesn't care.
- I was born fat.
- I hate Mondays.
- I'm tired all the time.
- I couldn't buy a relationship.
- No one appreciates me.
- He'll be a no show.
- Stupid meeting!
- No way!
- I hate computers.
- I'm no good.
- This always happens.
- This isn't worth it.
- I look terrible.
- I'm not creative.
- This is impossible.
- I'm not that good.
- I can't save any money.
- I'm too young.
- I'm always tired.
- Of all the rotten luck.
- Why me?
- I hate my job.
- My back always hurts.
- Why bother?
- I hate meetings.
- Ugh, another meeting.
- I blew it.
- I'm so stupid.
- I'm sick of this job.
- This gets me down.
- I hate my boss.
- They always want more.
- I'll never learn this!
- He's lucky; I'm not.
- I hate making decisions.
- I wouldn't hire myself.
- Nobody loves me.
- I have no pep.
- This is so boring.

The Anacondas in Life

Creating Positive Self-Talk

The best way to eliminate negative self-talk is to crowd out negative thoughts with positive self-talk and positive thoughts using phrases like the ones below. In team efforts you can substitute the words "we," "us," and "our" for "I," "me," and "my."

- Darn, I'm good.
- I can do this.
- I'm getting better.
- Someone has to be first.
- I'm a winner.
- I was born a champion.
- Life is good.
- I'm excited!
- Yes!!
- Positively!
- I'm looking good!
- Good and getting better!
- Thank goodness it's Monday!
- I'm all I have, but I'm all I need.
- I will not fail.
- What can we celebrate?
- What can go right does.
- Why not me?
- I'm the best, baby, the best.

- I feel great!
- I will do this.
- I'm unstoppable.
- I deserve this.
- I am on a roll.
- I expect to win and will.
- This looks good to me.
- Sounds terrific!
- I am the greatest!
- Fantastic!
- I feel good!
- Never say never.
- Here I am day!
- I cannot fail.
- How could I lose?
- So good I can't stand it.
- I'm invincible.
- Looking good!
- I expect good luck.

Yes, You Are Creative

An example of how people program themselves to underachieve is the phrase, "I am not creative."

By saying this repeatedly, we program ourselves to believe we are not creative and we instruct ourselves to act that way. We do not offer new ideas, think of new alternatives, take risks, or experiment.

Consider the "I am not creative" phrase. Every single day, we tear down and rebuild millions of cells in our bodies. The reality is if we were not constantly re-*creating* ourselves, we would die.

Therefore, to say, "I am not creative" is not only destructive, it is also incorrect. The same is true of mental creativity. The more we say, "I am not creative," the less creative we act.

Strategies for Improving Your Self-Talk

Before you can replace negative thoughts with positive thoughts, you must recognize those negative words and phrases and take steps to cast them out.

First, identify the specific words you say or think. Listen carefully to your self-talk for a day or two. Jot down the negative words and phrases you use. Then consciously decide not to use those words again by selecting replacement words to use instead.

If you make a habit of saying, "I don't have enough time," you have recorded those instructions on a memory chip playing in your head. Imagine replacing the words "I don't have enough time" with "I'll find time" on that memory chip. The old track is gone. All you hear is the new track. You never hear or say those negative words again.

Another way to eliminate negative self-talk is to write down the negative words you say and physically tear them up and throw them away. This reinforces your commitment to banish those words from your thoughts.

Examples of Turning Negative Thoughts into Positive Thoughts

Here are a few examples of how to transform thoughts and words from negative to positive.

Making a presentation

Negative: "I did okay on my presentation, but I could have done better."

Positive: "That was great! I gave a pretty good presentation and now I know what to do to be even better next time."

Having gained weight

Negative: "I look like a whale in this outfit."

Positive: "When I get home I am going to hang this outfit on my closet door and let it remind me daily how important my healthy exercise and eating plans are."

Getting a date turndown

Negative: "I felt like such a jerk asking her for a date and having her say, 'Are you serious?'"

Positive: "Well, I gave it a shot. I'm sure I will find someone who will be fun to be with."

Create and Use Positive Triggers

Another way to acquire a positive self-talk habit is to use positive trigger phrases. These snappy upbeat statements can stimulate positive energy and action. Two examples are below, but you can create your own.

Tabula Rasa!

I use Tabula Rasa! to give myself a fresh beginning each day and any other time I need it. Tabula Rasa is Latin for erased tablet. When I say or think, "Tabula Rasa!" I imagine wiping the slate clean in my life. Tabula Rasa! allows me to leave yesterday's mistakes, problems, challenges, setbacks, and obstacles behind. When I say Tabula Rasa! I instantly get a surge of hope and feel better about the future.

"I am the greatest!"

Muhammad Ali reinforced his own confidence and belief in his abilities by saying, "I am the greatest" repeatedly to himself and others.

Once Ali believed he was the greatest, he started acting and boxing that way. Eventually he became the most recognized personality on earth, the greatest!

The Anacondas in Life

You and Your Negative Self-Talk
Dos and Don'ts

Do:

- Eliminate all of your negative or limiting self-talk and replace it with positive self-talk.

- Listen to what you think and say, and identify negative thoughts you should caste out permanently.

- Create and use a positive trigger phrase like, "Wow, what a great day!"

- Give someone a hug.

- Remember you are what you think to yourself.

- Think and speak in a positive manner at all times.

Don't:

- Say things like "I'm not creative" that express untrue and distorted limitations about yourself.

- Say things like "I'm tired all the time" because that programs you to be tired all the time.

Method is more important than strength,
when you wish to control your enemies.
By dropping golden beads near a snake,
a crow once managed to have a passer-
by kill the snake for the beads.

—Henry Wadsworth Longfellow

Strategies for
Defeating the Anacondas

Obstacles are like wild animals. They are cowards but they will bluff you if they can. If they see you are afraid of them . . . they are liable to spring upon you; but . . . if you look them squarely in the eye, they will slink out of sight.

—Orison Swett Marden

Create an Anaconda-Free Zone

TAKE TIME TO think about the environment you are living and working in currently, and take steps to create an *Anaconda-Free Zone* at work, at home, and every where else you can.

To create an Anaconda-Free Zone, take steps to eliminate or avoid the Anacondas in your life. Then surround yourself with positive, nurturing influences.

Get Rid of the Anacondas in Your Life

The first strategy for creating an Anaconda-Free Zone is to get rid of the Anacondas in your life.

While it may not be practical or possible to dump them all, you should take steps to minimize the time you spend with negative influences.

A business owner said, "Your employees are either helping you or hurting you. Your job is to encourage the ones that are helping you and deal with the ones who are hurting you." I recommend a similar approach for the people in your life. Answer questions like these:

- Are the people in my life helping me, or are they hurting me?

- Are my family members, friends, and co-workers encouraging me to achieve my dreams and potential, or are they discouraging me and holding me back?

Take action to eliminate or limit the time you spend with Anacondas who are hurting you and holding you back. Replace them with mentors and friends who look out for your best interests and want you to succeed.

This is not easy. It is hard to detach from long-time "friends." It is even harder to distance yourself from co-workers, and it can be a huge challenge to break away from family member Anacondas.

One individual said that when she started eliminating the Anacondas in her life she soon realized she had very few true friends. "I'm down to a handful of friends now," she said. "But these are true friends."

Don't Allow Anyone to Humiliate or Abuse You

The *Washington Post* ran an article, "A Devastating Loss of Self-Esteem," where girls told how boys devalued and humiliated them. The article described boys who went up to girls right in their face and made degrading remarks, yet the girls still went out with the boys.

Whether a boy humiliates and makes fun of a girl or a girl does the same to a boy, it is wrong. The people being mean and cruel are Anacondas.

I recommend getting rid of any Anacondas like these in your life and finding someone who is kind and good with a loving heart. This can be hard to do, but you must avoid mean people if you want to be happy.

Marti the Bully Manager

A HALF HOUR after Paula started her new job she asked Marti, her manager, a question. Marti answered but seemed annoyed.

An hour later, Paula asked Marti, "Do you have a minute for another question?"

"Is this a 911 call or is this a 411 call?" Marti snapped.

This was only the beginning. Each day Marti became meaner and seemed to enjoy striking out to intimidate Paula. It came to a head when Marti threw letters Paula had typed into the air. "Wrong paper, missy!" she yelled.

Paula discussed this with her father. He said, "You can't change people like Marti and life's too short to put up with them. You don't have to work for someone like that."

Paula quit the next day and left Marti, the Anaconda, in her past.

Change Jobs to Avoid Anacondas?

Many people ask what to do if they have to work with Anacondas every day.

We spend more time at work than we do with friends or loved ones. When we are not happy at work, our work unhappiness spills into our personal lives.

Therefore, when people tell me they are very unhappy at work or their work environment is horrible, I know a major change is required.

If individuals find themselves in extremely negative work environments, there may be no solution but to change jobs. However, changing jobs is a significant step and I would not take it without looking for and considering alternatives.

Enough with the Bad News

Each day a tsunami of bad news bombards you nonstop. You cannot buy groceries without someone telling you about the latest scandals, disasters, or threats. The crawl at the bottom of the television provides a continuous bad news feed.

Cut back on your consumption of bad news and replace it with positive activities. Don't worry about being kept informed. If they discover a new continent, someone will tell you.

Tell Others about the Anacondas

Tell your co-workers, friends, and family members about the Anaconda concepts. Display one of our *Anaconda-Free Zone* posters in your work area, dorm, or home to remind people not be an Anaconda. They help.

Try the "ssssss" technique. "Ssssss" is the hiss of a snake about to strike. After you have told others about the Anacondas, the next time someone makes an

Anaconda-comment go "ssssss!" in a friendly manner. Saying "ssssss" may seem silly, but it works. People often act like Anacondas and do not realize it. By giving them a "ssssss" with a friendly smile, you can remind them pleasantly.

I only recommend using the "ssssss" technique with friends and trusted co-workers.

Do not say "ssssss" to hard-core aggressive Anacondas. They could react with anger.

Create a Nurturing Network

Take steps to create a nurturing network.

- Stay in touch with positive friends and family members who are upbeat and successful.
- Hang out with people who are trying to develop, grow, and be excellent.
- Go places where you can meet and get to know people who have high aspirations and goals.

Listen to Motivational Music

Music affects your attitude and outlook. Music is powerful because it sticks in your brain easily.

If you play negative songs repeatedly, you are hurting yourself. Somber tunes with dark lyrics are depressing. Certain kinds of rap music put people down, women particularly. Lyrics that shout complaints and insults are not good for anyone.

If you play positive songs, you are helping yourself. Upbeat music with inspiring lyrics lifts your spirits and energy. People listen to music when they exercise because it raises their energy level.

Taking Control as Manager

What should a manager or owner do if there is an Anaconda in the organization?

I try to give an individual the benefit of the doubt and work with a person who is acting like an Anaconda. Unfortunately, some Anacondas are determined to stay that way. You do not want Anacondas in your organization or on your team. In such cases, counsel them to other opportunities.

The president of a company called the day after hearing my talk on Anacondas. I asked why he was so happy. He said, "It was your talk on the Anacondas."

"My talk on Anacondas made you happy?" I said.

"No, not your talk," he said. "I fired two Anacondas this morning. After hearing you, I realized I had been putting up with these two people for a long time. I decided we all needed to be able to come to work and be happy. I bit the bullet and fired them both. I feel great!"

> *If you see a snake, just kill it – don't appoint a committee on snakes.*
>
> —Ross Perot

Create an Anaconda-Free Zone
Dos and Don'ts

Do:

- Create an Anaconda-Free Zone.
- Get rid of the serious Anacondas in your life or find ways to minimize the time you spend with them.
- Surround yourself with positive, nurturing people who want you to succeed.
- Put up an Anaconda-Free Zone poster.
- Give the "ssssss" technique a try.
- Take control of your self-talk.
- Manage your environment.

Don't:

- Allow yourself to speak or think negative thoughts.
- Allow anyone to bully you.
- Allow anyone to be mean or nasty to you.
- Hang on to friendships and relationships with people who are hurting you and not helping you.
- Allow Anacondas at work to erode the attitude and performance of the team.

*Hope is the key ingredient for all
happiness. You cannot be happy without
hope for the next moments in life. When
you give someone hope, you give them
happiness and a reason for living.*

—Jim Ball

Be a Peddler of Hope

MOST PEOPLE agree that the best defense can be a good offense. This is true when fighting Anacondas.

A powerful strategy for defeating Anacondas is to become a *Peddler of Hope*. A Peddler of Hope is someone who thinks and acts the opposite of each of the six Anaconda types and who goes into each day trying to find the best in others and help them succeed.

Be a Dream Sower

Instead of being an Anaconda Dream Snatcher, be a Dream Sower and encourage people to dream, think big, and pursue their potential.

- Encourage people to pursue their dreams.
- Tell individuals to think big.
- Push people to raise their sights.

Be a Possibility Thinker

Instead of being an Anaconda Limitation Thinker, be a Possibility Thinker and focus on what can be done and might be possible.

- Think outside the box to find new ideas.
- Take some risks and expand your experiences and contacts to open up new horizons.
- Look on the bright side.
- Make the most of what you have.

Spread Hope and Belief

Instead of being an Anaconda of Doubt and Despair, spread Hope and Belief and look forward to all the positive results that can be achieved.

- Say "Yes, I can" and "Yes, we can."
- Tell people you appreciate them.
- Reward and recognize efforts and results.
- Put fun into what you are doing.
- Be a steppingstone, not a stumbling block.
- Never say die.
- Have no doubt.
- Act with confidence.

Think Deservedness

Instead of being the Anaconda of Undeservedness, become a champion of Deservedness. Proclaim that you and your team deserve the things you want and are willing to work to get.

- Say "I am the greatest" or "we are the greatest."
- Picture yourself getting exactly what you want.
- Create and hold mental images of yourself after you achieve what you want to achieve.

Be a Motivator

Instead of being an Anaconda Demotivator, be a Motivator who walks around spreading positive energy, enthusiasm, and joy.

- Cheer people onward and upward.
- Tell others you believe in them and want them to win.
- Get excited.
- Pick up the pace.
- Be an encourager. Say "nice try," "good job," and "that's great."

Be a Positive You

Instead of being a Negative You Anaconda, be a Positive You and replace all your negative thoughts and words with positive self-talk and thoughts.

- Say "It's Sunny and 70!"
- Smile! Move briskly!
- Think enthusiasm!
- If you cannot say something nice or encouraging, do not say anything.
- Take time each day to reflect on what you have to be thankful for.

The Right Words at the Right Time

American Idol, the popular TV show, gives an example of using the right words at the right time to encourage others.

Of the show's judges, Randy Jackson, Paula Abdul, and Simon Cowell, Simon Cowell had a reputation for being the toughest judge.

In one situation, however, Randy and Paula jumped on a female contestant with critical comments. It was unusual for them to be so harsh and cold.

When it came time for Simon's critique the contestant was struggling to smile and not cry. Simon paused a moment. I am certain the young woman thought he, too, would be harsh.

Simon surprised me. He said, "Well, I don't know, I thought it was pretty good. I don't know what Paula and Randy were watching, but you look great and did a pretty good job."

I felt certain Simon sensed the situation and went out of his way to be positive so the young woman would not have her spirit broken. In that instant, he was a Peddler of Hope. The young woman did not win, but she left with confidence, thanks in part to Simon's right words at the right time.

Be a Peddler of Hope
Dos and Don'ts

Do:

- Be a Peddler of Hope.
- Decide to be a positive force in nature.
- Protect you own positive attitude.
- Be a Dream Sower.
- Be a Possibility Thinker.
- Spread Hope and Belief.
- Think Deservedness.
- Be a Motivator.
- Be a Positive You.
- Focus forward and upward to the future.

Don't:

- Focus on past mistakes and disappointments.
- Talk down to yourself.
- Be an Anaconda to anyone for any reason.

A danger foreseen is half avoided.
　　　　　　　　—Author unknown

Live Defensively

MOST PEOPLE agree that it is important to drive defensively. There are even courses that teach you how to be on the lookout for dangerous conditions and how to react to avoid obstacles and prevent accidents.

I recommend a similar approach for avoiding and preventing the negative impact of Anacondas.

Live Defensively and React Quickly

Be on the lookout for Anacondas so you can avoid them. Learn to react quickly and properly when Anacondas attack.

The biggest difference between winners and people who want to be winners but are not (wannabes) is how winners react to Anacondas. Winners have reflex responses to repel Anacondas. Wannabes do not. Winners have mastered defense techniques to stop Anacondas from dampening their enthusiasm. Wannabes have not. Winners overcome the attacks of Anacondas quickly. Wannabes do not.

First Reaction Is Key

The critical strategy for defensive living is to have a pre-planned good first reaction to an advancing Anaconda. This is like learning defensive driving techniques for preventing accidents in potentially dangerous conditions.

For example, my Dad taught me to take my foot off the accelerator and start slowing down the instant I see brake lights in front of me. When I see brake lights ahead, I react fast and automatically begin slowing down. This tip has helped me avoid accidents.

Since you do not know how or when an Anaconda might strike, you have to learn how to manage your reactions when it does attack. You cannot control others, but you must control yourself.

How are you going to react the next time someone shoots down your idea? What are you going to do when someone sends you a searing email criticizing your work? If a co-worker turns the conversation into a nasty gripe session, what will you do? How will you respond when a relative cuts you off as you are telling everyone at the table about your promotion?

Think about the situations and Anacondas you encounter and develop and practice using planned responses. This way you will have a good defense and not be caught off guard.

Just Leave

The best technique for avoiding Anacondas and minimizing their effect is to leave.

I have walked into a room, sensed negativity the moment I entered, and walked right out. I find some way to turn around and be out of there fast. In some cases, I have said nothing and just walked out.

Sometimes I use a pre-planned approach. A man who is a complainer and whiner used to seek me out to sit beside me during luncheon meetings so he could tell me his woes. Now when I go to these meetings I prearrange whom I will sit with.

More Tips for Living Defensively

Here are several additional ideas to consider.

- Hold onto your dreams no matter what others may do or say.
- Try changing subjects to avoid conversations that are negative or limiting in nature.
- Don't take it personally.
- Never lose your temper, erupt, or go into a rage.
- Do not try to convince die-hard Anacondas they are wrong. It is a waste of time.
- Avoid and do not participate in griping, complaining, and gossiping sessions.

Try Some Resistance

While I do not recommend getting into an argument with an Anaconda, sometimes Anacondas will back off right away if you resist their attack.

In a board meeting to discuss raising money for a charity, Gerald suggested we reduce our goal to something "more realistic and in line with our resources." He went on to argue that a smaller goal was not only more acceptable, it was "more prudent for us, as board members, to behave in a responsible manner."

This kind of Limitation-Thinking comment can squash any goal if you let it. Gerald was trying to put a monkey on our backs because we were being too aggressive and optimistic to suit him.

After a moment's silence another board member said, "Oh, I don't know Gerald, I think we would be irresponsible to go for a lower goal when more is possible. Wouldn't you rather shoot high and miss a bit than shoot low and hit?"

Gerald pondered a minute and said, "You are right. Let's go with the bigger goal we have."

There are no hard and fast rules. Use judgment and pick your battles. Do not try to back down every Anaconda you encounter. However, do not let people run over you. Stand up for what you believe.

Keep Your Dreams to Yourself

I do not share my dreams and goals with anyone who is not going to help me pursue and achieve them.

There are people who would not want us to achieve our dreams if they knew what our dreams are. Maybe they would be jealous. Perhaps they would want us to stay like them and not move ahead. Whatever the reasons might be, I do not want anyone wishing or hoping I do not achieve what I want to achieve. Therefore, I keep my dreams and goals to myself.

The Anacondas in Life

Live Defensively
Dos and Don'ts

Do:

- Think through the first reactions you can use to fend off Anacondas.

- Share your dreams with people who want you to achieve them and who can help you turn them into realities.

- Put one foot in front of the other and begin to make small changes.

- Stand up for what you value and believe.

Don't:

- Share your dreams with anyone who might not want you to achieve them.

- Allow a little initial resistance to keep you from pursuing big goals.

Growing up does not mean we cast aside our childhood dreams. Growing up means being able to pursue those dreams and make them bigger and better. Dreams are not like clothing we grow out of. You were not born to grow out of your dreams; you were born to grow into them.

—Jim Ball
from *Soar . . . If You Dare*

The Anacondas in Life

Dare to Dream!

Here are the three most important messages in this book to remember and apply so you can achieve your dreams.

First, **you are greater than you think you are.** The greatest miracle in your life is not going to come in the years ahead; it is already here. *You* are the greatest miracle in your life, and what a wonderful miracle you are! You have the potential for greatness. You can achieve and become all you desire. You do not have to wait to learn anything or do anything; you can begin right now to fulfill your destiny.

Second, **live defensively to avoid or defeat the Anacondas you will encounter.** Do not allow the Anacondas to deter you, distract you, crush your hope, or limit your dreams and aspirations. Do not let the Anacondas make you question yourself or your ability to turn your dreams into realities. You can do what must be done. Trust in yourself, for you are a miracle.

Third, **dream big dreams and pursue them.** Life is the ultimate gift. With it comes the power and ability to decide what you will become through the choices you make and the dreams you pursue. Choose big dreams to release the full power of your spirit so we all may see the greatness and wonder you have brought to our earth.

If you ever need to lift your spirits and begin anew, just say Tabula Rasa! and let the magic begin.

You are a true miracle. Greatness can be yours.

About the Authors

James Ball is CEO and Jennifer Kuchta (cook-ta) is Vice President of The Goals Institute, the company they founded to help organizations and individuals achieve their potential through goal achievement.

Jim and Jennifer write books, develop learning programs, and provide speeches and seminars for organizations.

Previously, Jim co-founded and was CEO of Venture America, a venture capital firm that helped launch more than twenty companies, including The Discovery Channel. Before that, he was a managing partner at Arthur Andersen. Jim is a certified public accountant. He has been an adjunct faculty member at George Mason University where he co-founded and was the first president of GMU's Entrepreneurial Institute.

Jim and his wife Dolly live in Virginia. They have two adult daughters, Jennifer and Stephanie, and two grandsons, Ryan and Tyler.

Previously, Jennifer oversaw finance, administration, investor relations, and services and support of portfolio companies at Venture America. Before that, she was a marketing specialist for fine arts. She has an accounting degree and is the publisher for all works produced by The Goals Institute.

Books by the Authors

Keep It Simple for Success® is a series of books and learning programs authored and developed by Jim Ball and Jennifer Kuchta and published by The Goals Institute. The titles in the series as of the date of publication of this book are:

- ABCs for Life
- It's About TIME!
- Professionalism *Is* for Everyone
- The Anacondas in Life
- World-Class Customer Service

Jim also has written these books:

- Soar . . . If You Dare®
- DNA Leadership through Goal-Driven Management
- The Entrepreneur's Tool Kit

Seminars and Train-the-Trainer Resources

The Goals Institute provides seminars and train-the-trainer resources on the contents of this book and the other books above. If you would like more information, please contact us.

Join Anaconda Free!

WE HOPE this book and the ideas we have suggested help you identify and overcome any Anacondas in Life you may encounter.

To help you ward off the Anacondas that slither your way, we invite you to join Anaconda Free!

Please visit us online to learn more and to download your free Anaconda Free! poster and other goodies.

www.anacondafree.com

General Contact Information

To learn more about our books, volume discounts, seminars, and train-the-trainer tools, please contact us:

The Goals Institute

703-264-2000

www.goalpower.com

www.goalsinstitute.com

www.kissbooks.com

email: info@goalsinstitute.com